S0-ABD-614

Soul Be Free:
Poems, Prose, & Prayers

My Sister...
I thank God for the gift in you to my brother...
Yo'r Brother Friend
Tony

Soul Be Free:
Poems, Prose, & Prayers

by
ALFONSO WYATT
and
OUIDA C. WYATT

Sisterfriend,
Godspeed as your Journey into Self.
Love, OUIDA

Soul Be Free:
Poems, Prose, & Prayers

Copyright © 2010
by Alfonso & Ouida C. Wyatt

cover design by Trish Hadley

All rights reserved. No part of this book may be used or reproduced in any manner whatsoever without written permission from the publisher, except in the case of brief quotations embodied in articles and reviews.

Published by

THE POWER OF HOPE PRESS
6137 East Mescal Street
Scottsdale, Arizona 85254-5418

ISBN: 978-1-932842-38-8 — $ 12.95

The Power of Hope Press seeks to publish books drawn from actual life experiences that educate, edify, and inspire.

Printed in the United States of America

FOREWORD
Derek H. Suite, M.D.

Ever listen to a piece of music, or spend several minutes mesmerized by an exquisite work of art and experience a feeling of well being? That's exactly the kind of feeling *Soul Be Free* evokes! A feeling that transcends our current reality, seeps into our DNA, moves past our ego defenses, and touches our soul-place. *Soul Be Free* taps a healing force from deep within — a force that somehow uses the broken pieces of our lives and the power of personal reflection to build an internal lighthouse of hope, triumph, and strength, no matter how dark the external reality we face. *Soul Be Free* is about liberation power within each of us that alters how we process and cope with the vicissitudes of life. As Hemingway accurately observed, "The world breaks everyone, and afterward, many are strong at the broken places."

In my years as a psychiatrist, leading Full Circle Health, an organization devoted to healing the psychological and spiritual wounds of children and families, I have discovered that we are challenged daily to find strength in broken places. In light of the ever growing economic strain we, as a society, are becoming increasingly aware that we are inextricably linked to our neighbor more so through suffering than through the World Wide Web. It is in this context that *Soul Be Free* comes to us as a "healing technology." Its gifted and sensitive authors communicate a divine message that offers a unique pathway to new hope and wellness. This work is sure to illuminate the parts of our souls that long to make contact with abundant joy, inner peace, ageless wisdom and the healing force of love.

The raw beauty of *Soul Be Free's* prescription for healing lies in its authors enlightened understanding and passion for living an examined and fulfilled life. As ministers, teachers and overcomers, Alfonso and Ouida Wyatt are uniquely qualified to lead us to the secret place where liberated souls roam free. As the great Nelson Mandela puts it: "*There is nothing like returning to a place that remains unchanged to find the ways in which you yourself have altered.*" Dear wearied, wounded and worried soul, I urge you to read, reflect, and rest in your freedom.

—DEREK H. SUITE, M.D., Founder and CEO
Full Circle Health, PLLC

Table of Contents

THE MIND

THE ISSUES

THE RELATIONSHIP

THE SOUL

THE BENEDICTION

*Poems in lower case are by A. Wyatt
 and poems in UPPER CASE are by O.C.W.

TO OUR FAMILY
WITH LOVE

THE MIND

i think i feel i feel i think

the power to feel what's in the heart
given to all but unequal in part
some feel the strength
in a mighty surge
like an emotional fireball
about to emerge
while others have to
endlessly wait
for feelings that always
come too late
is emotion a thought
first from the mind
which then directs our
actions in kind
or
is it the feeling which
actually comes first
releasing an energy
to be dispersed
feelings about thoughts
a paradoxical start
thoughts about feelings
from
the
mind
or
the
heart

Have you ever experienced inner confusion — not sure of what you are thinking or feel that you think too much? What we experience internally is eventually made manifest externally. This dilemma, when assigned societal influenced gender roles, usually renders women as too emotional and men as too rational — one lost in feelings and the other bound by thoughts. I admit that I have struggled with my thoughts about my feelings. This internal dialogue can go on and on *ad nauseam*; playing itself out in a variety of scenarios which only serve to heighten emotional intensity — and creating more thoughts (or is it the same thought?). Feelings and thoughts, like left handedness and right handedness, exist within us all. Our inner pursuit is not to rely exclusively on thoughts or always default to feelings, but rather struggle to find a workable balance.

He who gets wisdom loves his own soul; he [she] who cherishes understanding prospers. —Proverbs 19:8

this place

there
is this place
i want to go
where only positive
energies flow
looking toward
the void of space
trying to project
myself to this place
there is no real
direction to take
yet go I must
can not forsake
this chance to take
a solo flight
vanish into
the starry night
pass all we know
in our world
pass the milky way
celestial swirl and the sun's
warming light
beyond comets
ordained flight
this night
decided time to go

when this thought
interrupted my cosmic flow
this place may be beyond the last star
or it
may be
wherever
you
are

I have been intrigued by the mind since my youth. It was amazing to me that people could think thoughts not known to others. I discovered that the mind can either be a person's best friend or worst enemy. A mind mired in disappointment and bitterness can only produce bitter disappointment. A mind fixated on one thing will miss possible mind-changing opportunities. An over-imaginative mind has the power to defy the laws of physics by bouncing between the past, present and future–or live in all three states at the same time. The desire to constantly escape from an undesired place or reality, while understandable to some extent is not helpful in the long run. The journey to nowhere always exacts a dire price on the traveler's time, quality of life and ability to solve problems in a real and lasting way.

Where can I go from your Spirit? Where can I flee from your presence? If I go to the heavens, you are there; If I make my bed in the depths, you are there. If I rise on the wings of dawn, if I settle on the far side of the sea, even there your right hand will guide me, your right hand will hold me fast. Psalm 139:7-10

into self

be still

all must be still

hear the sound

faint heartbeat

poised to descend

the inner abyss

jagged edge

blinding darkness

endless as eternity

fate awaits

fear shouts

stay safe

protect the being

from further pain

doubts conspire

giving birth to

more questions

now here i stand

wrapped in naked truth

spirit and will collide

soul tears

fall

frail wings

ripped

by discouraging winds

yet still

i

plunge

What do you do when you are a stranger to yourself? Can you be sure that what you say about you is the truth; or do you tell yourself convincing lies in a desperate attempt to fool truth? Where do you turn for honest feedback when everyone around you has bought into your manufactured false image? What happens when you have more nagging questions about yourself than reassuring answers? Who can comfort the real you?

For I know the thoughts and plans that I have for you, says the Lord, thoughts and plans for welfare and peace and not for evil, to give you hope in your final outcome. Jeremiah 29:11

WHAT'S ON YOUR MIND
WHEN YOU'RE OUT OF YOUR MIND?

WHAT'S ON YOUR MIND
WHEN YOU'RE OUT OF YOUR MIND?

ARE YOU HIDING FROM REALITY
OR IS THIS REALITY YOU?
ARE THOUGHTS AND FEELINGS
A SPEEDING TRAIN WITH NO BRAKES
WHERE YOUR HEART IS BROKEN
AND JUST PLAIN ACHES?

WHAT'S ON YOUR MIND
WHEN YOU'RE OUT OF YOUR MIND?

ARE YOU IN A HOUSE OF HORRORS WHERE
EVERY DOORWAY IS DARK,
EVERY STEP A TRAP,
WHERE YOU
CANNOT TAKE ANOTHER THING
DROPPED IN YOUR LAP?
IS THE WORLD NOW
FACETED, CHISELED, WARPED
NO LONGER COMPARTMENTALIZED
IN YOUR EYES?

YOU'VE TAKEN A TRIP AND
WE'VE WATCHED YOU GO
IF YOU RETURN

THERE'S ONE THING WE MUST KNOW
WHAT'S ON YOUR MIND
WHEN YOU'RE
OUT OF
YOUR
MIND?

The vicissitudes of life can create a chasm between situations and our reactions to them. There are times when the stresses of life have us reacting before we give ourselves the opportunity to see beyond what we are facing. We cannot transcend a problem that we become a part of. There are times when we do this unwittingly and there are times when we make the choice to hide behind the smoke and mirrors of delusion and denial. At each fork in the road of challenge there is an opportunity to be swept away by emotion or focused enough to hear the still small voice of grace. Try it the next time when facing a trying circumstance—and before you space out call out to the God of your constant help.

For God did not give us the Spirit of fear, but of power and love, and of a sound mind. 2 Timothy 1:7

metamorphosis

remember
those nights
oh how you
cried
voices said
time to
decide
live and grow
on
a different plane
or allow
your life
to stay the
same
the struggle for self
a peculiar
fight
lines are drawn
no wrong or
right
now closer to
the moment
when
the butterfly
struggles
to
ascend

The voice of change can only be heard by the living–yet it is the living that ignores the faint whisper or loud shout. Your "change perspective" is formed by your history of coping with or avoiding change. Some people want to challenge change but never commit to change. It is possible to declare a truce with the unlovable parts of self thereby ignoring the need to grow. Change is a necessary catalyst for transformation; but here is the caveat–just because you struggle to change does not mean that you automatically have been transformed. Beloved, work hard on the ignored inner strongholds that have up to this point, defied change and by extension, frustrate your transformation.

And do not be conformed to this world but be transformed by the renewing of your mind, that you may prove what is good and acceptable and perfect will of God. Romans 12:2

A Prayer for the Mind

Oh Lord, you taught that the 1ˢᵗ Commandment in scripture is to love You with all of our heart, our soul and mind. Give us courage to be utterly directed by you. No one knows the creation better than the creator therefore I focus my mind on you. I make it my sole intention to move by your leading. As the caterpillar sheds its cocoon in order to be the butterfly that will take flight, we must turn from fear and doubt putting all our faith and trust in you. Every natural experience yields a spiritual lesson. Help me to grow from all I go through in my life journey. This is my prayer. Amen

THE ISSUES

HERE I AM

HERE I AM IN MY LIFE SPACE
WITH ALL THAT I COULD POSSIBLY BE
A RICH DEPOSIT
OF
GIFTS IN ME

THERE WAS A TIME
WHEN IT WAS IN MY MIND
I SHOULD PICK ONE THING
THAT WOULD DEFINE ME
BUT HOW ABSURD
HOW CAN IT BE
THAT I SHOULD PICK
A PART OF ME

HERE I AM IN MY LIFE SPACE
WITH NO FEAR
I MUST BE FREE
TO EXPLORE
AND
EMBRACE
EVERY GIFT
INSIDE
OF ME

I MUST BE STRONG
TAKE MY PLACE
MARK THIS WORLD
WITH GIFTS BY GRACE
A SHINING
LIGHT
MY
LIFE SPACE

I am the expression of God in the earth. It is His hand that has fashioned me and what the Creator has deposited in me has been there from the beginning of time. Each day is an opportunity to remove all preconceived notions of what I should be and be present to the present. My gifts, my talents and my passions reflect God's grace in my life. I must allow each season of my life to be an expression of God's precious treasure that is within me.

But we have this treasure in earthen vessels, that the excellency of the power may be of God and not of us. 2 Corinthians 4:7

FRUSTRATION COMING & GOING

FRUSTRATION TAKES HOLD
TIGHTENING AROUND ME
CLOSING IN ON ME

FRUSTRATION TAKES HOLD
GRIPPING ME, SQUEEZING ME
FRUSTRATING ME

FRUSTRATION TAKES HOLD
SAPPING MY STRENGTH
FROM THE INSIDE OUT MY THOUGHTS
FROM THE OUTSIDE IN
MY MOOD

I MUST LOOK TO THE HILLS
AND NOT MY TORMENTOR
NOT LISTEN TO FRUSTRATION
BUT HEAR THE VOICE
OF HOPE DOWN DEEP

MY IDENTITY IS NOT THIS THING
IT IS A SOUL IN FLIGHT
I MUST FOCUS INWARD ON
THE CALM,
THE PEACE,
THE LIGHT

SPIRIT LIFTING, SPIRIT MOVING, SPIRIT GIVING,
SPIRIT FREEING

FRUSTRATION IS GOING
NOT COMING TO STAY
AN INNER CHALLENGE
FROM DAY TO DAY

FRUSTRATION DISSOLVED
BY LOVE DIVINE
A REDEEMING PRESENCE
THAT WILL KEEP MY MIND

There are times in our lives when we feel totally frustrated by the feeling that we are not progressing in our personal or professional life: the feeling that we cannot seem to complete things that we start; the feeling that there are just not enough hours in the day; the feeling that we are always fighting an up hill battle. Well the fact is that frustration is a feeling we have but is not who we are. Our triumph is in knowing who we are and who's we are. Our victory is in believing that we are conquerors in God over all frustration.

For we are God's workmanship, created in Christ Jesus to do good works, which God has prepared in advance for us to do. Ephesians 2:10

without hope

would you say the worse
place to be
in a state where you're
not free
to express your thoughts
and feelings inside
trapped in a role
can no longer abide
how is it to feel there is no love
as you slowly sink trying to stay above
never thinking
there is a brighter day
no ideas that can carry
you away
to the place where lost
dreams are found
kindling the spirit so
hope can abound

Some people think that hope is an emotion wasted solely on hopeless people. It must be said that hope devoid of action opens the door to dissatisfaction that can lead to crippling despair. Sometimes people are reticent to share their hopes with others; perhaps out of fear of being ridiculed, demeaned or misunderstood. Beloved hope is not an end point but a point of departure. It is hope that sustains a person when reason and doubt collide. It is hope that searches for a brighter day even when all seems dark. Hope is the vehicle that links desire to will. Hope is the energy needed to power the first steps toward a state of well being.

But those who hope in the Lord shall renew their strength. They will soar on wings like eagles; they will run and not grow weary, they will walk and not be faint. Isaiah 40:31

ANGER LOOMS IN MY ROOM

ANGER LOOMS
IN MY ROOM
SPIRITS SPEAK
SOUL IS
DOOMED
SEEPING IN
UNDER THE DOOR
PRESSING UPWARD
FROM THE FLOOR
WINDOWS STEAMED
WALLS NOW SWEAT
ROOM IS MISTY
CURTAINS WET
FILLING IN
AT EVERY STAGE
YEARS OF ANGER
HARBORED RAGE
MOVING IN
AND
OUT WITH ME
FORGIVING SPIRIT
IS THE KEY
OPEN DOOR
AND
FRESHEN AIR
CLEAR THE ROOM
DO
I
DARE?

Anger throws a blanket of negativity over you spiritually. It stifles any seeds of hope because it distracts from the moment at hand. Anger demands our attention and forms a barrier between you and your next life lesson. The reality is that if we do not release the anger we actually go from feeling stifled to carrying the oppressive weight of past hurts and unresolved issues. Do not let anger hinder your movement and impede your growth. Anger can not release itself, but it can be dispelled—forgiveness is the liberator.

For man's anger does not bring about the righteousness that God desires. James 1:20

the captor

another night
the captor sleeps
content knowing

                                 my
                                 dreams

shackled

                                 hopes

crushed

                                 mind

distracted
my cries of anguish
lost in empty rooms
strewn promises
buoyed by bitter tears
my
soul a prisoner
born of fate
convicted by destiny
these cursed bars
imprisons doom
keys of hope
lost
in endless options

this night my captor calls
desperation's prayers
at last heard

this very night

                                        the evil one

destroyed

                standing over the vanquished
                sweet victory in hand
                yet there is no joy
                for the captor
                me

There are people who are locked up but never served time in prison. The people I am referring to are self-sentenced to cells of anger, hate, bitterness, victimization, depression, fear and doubt. The self-incarcerated are free to go to work, family gatherings and yes — even to church. Yet, these same sisters and brothers return to cells where their dreams are shackled, hopes fettered and are inextricably bound to negative people, places and things. When a person is doing hard time, he or she may ask what power can lock me up even when I yearn to be free? This question, usually posed during isolated confinement, while profound, can not free a person from the dungeon of self. The desire to be free must be stronger than the fetters that bind the mind, heart and spirit.

Wait on the Lord, be of good courage and He shall strengthen your heart; wait, I say upon the Lord! Psalm 27:14

A Prayer For Issues

Oh God it feels like every step there is a trap set for me, tailored for my feet to step in. I really want to stay the course but at times I feel consumed by my circumstance, bogged down by everything that is going wrong. Help me get to a clearing. Help me sort out what is real from that which is false. Help me silence the negative dialogue inside of me. Help me forgive myself and others. Help me transcend hurt feelings by letting go of the past I can not change. Living for today means receiving with an open heart the love you have for me daily. Amen.

THE RELATIONSHIP

unity

fragile alliance
flower to stem
God married
both of them
beauty in union
must be shown
as one not made
to stand alone
some glory in
only the bloom
erroneous thought
don't leave room
to give the stem
credit due
for it sustains
and anchors
you

There is a dynamic relationship between what you show on the outside and what holds you together on the inside. It is probably more fun to focus on the external: how we look, how we are perceived by others, but if there is no grounding on the inside a person can be described as all show and no substance. I am reminded of how Hollywood can depict a grand mansion but a look behind the beautiful front yields an empty back lot — there is nothing there. A line from a song that the old folk would sing captures a timeless thought and suggestion: Be sure, be very sure that your anchor holds and grips the solid ground.

I am the vine, you are the branches. If a man remains in me and I in him, he will bear much fruit, apart from me you can do nothing. John 15:5

MY MAIN MAN

HIS ENDLESS LOVE
ONLY FOR ME
AND NOT THE OMNIPOTENT
ONE I SEE
MY MAIN MAN
NO LESS THAN GREAT
NO FEAR IN HIM
BEIN' STOPPED
AT HEAVEN'S GATE

SENSITIVE
CARING
FUN
THAT'S MY NUMBER ONE

JUST THAT THE CREATOR
DON'T FIT IN
EXCLUDING HIM
AIN'T NO REAL SIN

HOLDIN' BACK
ON THE ALMIGHTY
MY MAIN MAN FEELS GOOD
JUST HOLDIN' ME

PLANNIN' LIFE
AND
FEELIN' LOVE
JUST NO ROOM
FOR THE ONE ABOVE
MY MAIN MAN
CAN HANG WITH ME
BUT NOT THE GOD OF EARTH
SKY
AND
SEA?

From the beginning of time, as chronicled in the Holy Writ, we have known the works of God as seen throughout the earth, the sky and sea. We are privileged as human beings to know God and to be known by Him. As we look to God, our natural experiences yield spiritual lessons. The life we live before Him becomes an act of worship, therefore every relationship we engage in should make our Heavenly Father proud. As we look to God he will lead us, guide us, teach us that every choice we make has consequences. If the Creator is ignored, how can we ultimately grow in relationship to the created?

The heavens declare the glory of God; and the firmament shows His handiwork. Psalm 19:1

safe harbor

if we can not take love
truly professed
to another
then hopelessly
we are lost forlorn
sister
and
brother
cast adrift on
a friendless sea
sails
billowed by hate
evil wind
forever
blow
a wider void create
can we find together
some shelter
from the storm
rescue the words
i love you

a new bond form
this day
into forever
we sail this
turgid sea
who first
speak
the words find
safe harbor
in me

One can not count the number of poems, songs, books or movies inspired by love. It seems that the more we search for love, the more elusive love can become. Some people have tired of looking for love and have become satisfied with a "marked down" version of the real thing; while others fall for the idea of love and not its essence. If we lived forever and a day we would never fully reconcile both sides of love—a wonderful gift or a horrible present.

Love is patient, love is kind. It does not envy. It does not boast, it is not proud. It is not rude, it is not self-seeking, it is not easily angered, it keeps no record of wrongs. Love does not delight in evil but rejoices with truth. It always protects, it always trusts, always hopes, always perseveres. Love never fails. 1 Corinthians 13:4-8a

SISTER FRIEND

YOU'RE THE ONE WHO WILL COMFORT
ENCOURAGE AND CARE
THE ONE WHO WILL SPEAK TRUTH
THE PLAIN TRUTH
YOU DARE
YOU'RE THE ONE WHO CELEBRATES
REJOICING WITH ME
WHEN FLOOD WATERS RISE
WITHOUT WORDS
NEEDS YOU SEE
YOU'RE THE ONE WHO CAN GO
THE EXTRA MILE
WHEN AT MIDNIGHT
IT'S YOU
I JUST HAVE TO DIAL
FIRST YOU LISTEN
THEN GIVE FEEDBACK
HELPING ME REGAIN
THE RIGHT TRACK
I MAY NOT LIKE
WHAT YOU SAY
ALL THE TIME
BUT WITH ME
THE MOUNTAINS

YOU PATIENTLY CLIMB
YOU'RE MY SISTER FRIEND
THE BOND UNIQUE
EACH SEASON'S EXPRESSION
OUR TREASURE
TO KEEP

Friendships that are the most satisfying and central to our being are friendships that stand the test of time. Real relationship are the ones in which a conversation can end and six months later you can pick it up as if it were yesterday. It is the give-and-take, not the take, take, take that make us feel supported and safe. Take a close look at the girlfriends in your group and list the positives and negatives. Reflect on the truths of the connection: is the time spent inspiring or draining? Are you advised openly upon sharing or are you merely judged? Is the relationship edifying or do you dread the thought of the next get together? God has to teach us how to love those we say that we love.

A friend loves at all times, but a brother [sister] is born for adversity.
Proverbs 17:17

CAMP MEETING

WHEN WE GET TO THE CAMP MEETING WE'LL ALL
TAKE A TURN
A TURN TO TELL JUST HOW GOOD GOD IS
HOW HE SAW YOU THROUGH SINCE THE LAST
TIME WE GATHERED
THROUGH STORM CLOUDS GREAT AND SMALL

YOU'LL TELL HOW YOU KNELT IN PRAYER, HOW
YOU CRIED OUT BEFORE GOD AND HOW YOU
FELT HIS PRESENCE OR HIS ABSENCE
HOW YOU ALMOST LOST YOUR MIND AND HE
KEPT YOU
YES HE KEPT YOU FROM WHAT YOU WOULD
HAVE SAID OR WHAT YOU WOULD HAVE DONE
OR WHAT YOU WOULD HAVE SAID & DONE
JESUS KEPT YOU

WHEN WE GET TO THE CAMP MEETING WE'LL ALL
TAKE A TURN
GRANDMOTHER TAKE YOUR TURN AND TELL
HOW YOU NEVER THOUGHT YOU'D LIVE TO SEE
ALL YOU SEEIN'

MOTHERS TAKE YOUR TURN TO TELL HOW
YOU'VE COME THIS FAR BY FAITH, WATCHING
GOD MAKE A WAY OUT OF NO WAY
DAUGHTERS TAKE YOUR TURN CAUSE MOTHERS
LISTENING,

MOTHER IS LISTENING, LISTEN MOTHERS
SISTERS DON'T MISS OUT TAKE A TURN AND TELL
WHAT YOU'VE SEEN WHAT YOU'RE SEEING AND
HOW YA' SEE IT

IT'S A DIFFERENT WORLD OUT HERE
THE NEWS IS CRAWLING AT THE BOTTOM OF THE
TV, THOUGHTS ARE BLOGGED BY COMPUTER,
WITH TEXT MESSAGING VIA CELL PHONE, ALL IN
AN INSTANT
SIGNS OF CHANGING TIMES AND SEASONS

ONE MINUTE YOU'RE FEELING FINE THE NEXT
YOU'RE FEELING FLUSHED THE NEXT YOU FEEL
THE HEAT AND THE NEXT THERE'S A CHILL IN
THE AIR IS IT JUST ME?

AT THIS CAMP MEETING WE WILL ALL TAKE A
TURN TO TELL JUST HOW GOOD GOD IS
TELLING THE STORIES THAT MARK THE SEASONS
AND PLACE THE STONES IN THE ROAD FOR
GENERATIONS TO FOLLOW.

It has been said that each generation stands upon the shoulders of the previous one and that you can not know where you are going without knowing where you have come from. History records the test, the troubles and the triumphs of each by gone era. Our charge is to be part of history by telling our story without fear or shame. Telling the good, the not-so-good and the midnights of our days. Our stories become the stones in the road urging life travelers of all ages to stay in the race and never grow weary of fighting the good fight.

Even when I am old and gray, do not forsake me, O God, till I declare your power to the next generation, your might to all who are to come. Psalm 71:18

you

to be all you can
the noble goal
constantly growing
as truth unfold
eyes wide open
you travel the road
head held high
you carry your load
no fears that grip
or hold you back
gone is the need
to defend or attack
a person in all sense
of the word
the product of ideals
we all
have
heard

Life offers challenges but none more exciting than knowing that you can work on yourself. The opportunity for personal growth should never be viewed as a boring chore—or something to do tomorrow. The rewards you receive and energy you save by finding your authentic self is invaluable. When I wrote this poem some 25 years ago, I was coming into a deeper awareness of myself—not quite sure where I was headed but excited that I was going somewhere. I soon discovered that the destination was inward to a place called soul.

For the revelation waits an appointed time; it speaks of the end and will not prove false. Though it linger, wait for it; it will certainly come and will not delay. Habakkuk 2:3

A Prayer for Relationship

God, help us to love the people we say we love. Our capacity to sustain right relationships is sorely limited without you. Striking the right balance in any committed relationship is impossible without you. Our desire to be known and understood by others takes patience. We've got to be transparent in our sharing without shame or fear. Help us to develop the ability to be guided by insight and not spontaneous wants that overshadow our needs. Amen

THE SOUL

OUR DAILY BREAD

DAILY
DAWNING
IN MY SOUL
LORD OF LOVE
MAKE ME WHOLE

DAILY
DEVOTION
NEAR MY GOD TO THEE
WORSHIP AND PRAISE
RENEW
SET ME FREE

DAILY
DESIRE
THINK ON THESE THINGS
HONEST
JUST
PURE
INNER PEACE
IT BRINGS

DAILY
DOING
GUIDE MY FEET
LOVE LIGHT
SHINE ON
ALL I MEET

DAILY DRESSING
GOD'S ARMOR TO STAND
BREASTPLATE OF RIGHTEOUSNESS,
SWORD
OF SPIRIT
IN HAND

We need strength on a daily basis to realize the treasure within. God does not expect that we would be perfect because He is doing the perfecting work. He does expect that we would be active participants in seeking Him and growing in faith. We must trust that the Creator who has begun the good work within us will bring us to the fulfillment of our life's purpose. Just as we need bread for sustenance and exercise to stay physically fit our spiritual muscles can only be strengthened by affirming our faith daily.

Give us this day our daily bread. Matthew 6:11

soul search

this path for seekers
of the soul
virgin ground
leads to self

complacency

seductive siren of the mind

sings

to search is pain move no more

yield

but only to catch a resolute breath

now

cry for hope

or

moan

in sadness

your quest

carried by

a

whisper

one

more

step

It has been said that your life's purpose is to find your purpose. Where do you begin to look? How can you find your purpose when you don't know what it looks like or how it feels? Could you have walked by your purpose? Did you abort your purpose out of frustration? Are you prone to take daily polls from family, friends or strangers about your life and now find that you are aimlessly following the purpose of others? Have you read books on purpose and now you feel even more confused? True purpose can only be revealed through an intentional and dynamic relationship with God. So stop crying, moaning or being angry--it is time to take your inward journey, but this time you will walk with the Lord.

Trust in the Lord with all your heart, and lean not on your own understanding; in all your ways acknowledge Him, and he shall direct your path. Proverbs 3:5-6

who are you

i am comfort in the night
strength to go on and fight
can you see me...

i am spirit moving the wind
blowing troubles away my friend
can you see me...

i am wisdom now understand
cling to my all knowing hand
can you see me...

i am patience here to stay
helping seekers find their way
can you see me...

i am the calm in the storm
faith in love new bond form
can you see me...

i am all but not one
spirit
father
and son
can you see me...

It is easy to get caught up trying to make it on your own. This is especially true for people who have had to fight and claw their way through life. But every now and then a person is faced with a challenge that their strength can not conquer; their will can not bend nor can their best friends be of any help. It is in this time that one is forced to look past personal resources, favorite excuses, networking circles and admit the need for help from a greater power.

I will lift up my eyes to the hills—where does my help come from? My help comes from the Lord, the Maker of heaven and earth. Psalm 121:1-2

enlightenment

children of the light
heed this urgent call
use thine power
over darkness
stumble never fall
illume dark corners
in all hearts and minds
share this precious flame
the tie that binds
hatred is thine enemy
ignorance another foe
so band together small flames
wherever ye may go
there is strength in numbers
remember ye are light
and every flicker
a wound to darkness
this our eternal
fight

You are called to be a light in a world that has fallen in love with darkness. Do not hide your light or allow others to drain your light; do not consciously dim your beam in a misguided attempt to not outshine others. Do not slip into darkness by refusing to recharge your spiritual batteries through worship. And please know that you can not find your light spending your life in a dimly lit club. Your guiding light is not at the bottom of a bottle or in the arms of another person. Your Divine illumination is an unmerited gift from on High and is crafted to shine no matter the circumstance.

God is light in him there is no darkness at all... 1John 1:5b

GOD WITH US

IN THE BEGINNING WAS THE WORD, AND THE
WORD WAS WITH GOD, AND THE WORD WAS GOD.
HE WAS WITH GOD IN THE BEGINNING. *John 1:1-2*

Alpha and Omega in cosmic embrace
ends of time meet
The great star of the universe
herald the new born King
He rides upon the rhythm of time
Sing my soul sing

FOR TO US A CHILD IS BORN, TO US A SON IS
GIVEN, AND THE GOVERNMENT WILL BE ON HIS
SHOULDERS. AND HE WILL BE CALLED WONDER-
FUL COUNSELOR, MIGHTY GOD, EVERLASTING
FATHER, PRINCE OF PEACE. THE ZEAL OF THE
LORD ALMIGHTY WILL ACCOMPLISH THIS.
Isaiah 9:6-7

Miracle of miracles
Divine spirit
wrapped in earthly flesh
Born to wipe away
tears of the hurt,
the despised,
the lost
and
forsaken
His spirit transcends
time
and space

His spirit
a light that consumes
the world's darkness

And His spirit
a gift to one
and all
Sing
my
soul
sing

THE VIRGIN WILL BE WITH CHILD AND WILL GIVE
BIRTH TO A SON, AND THEY WILL CALL HIM
IMMANUEL—WHICH MEANS "GOD WITH US."
Matthew 1:22-23

Immanuel God with us
in the beginning
to the end of the age
The gift given
for our redemption,
giving to us
the abundant life
Wonderful counselor,
mighty God
Everlasting Father,
Prince of Peace
Immanuel God with us
in the beginning
to the end
of the age
Sing

my
soul
sing

This awesome Spirit evident from the beginning of time until time is no more is available to take residence in your soul. This Spirit can advise, chastise, encourage and illuminate every step along life's dark and unknown pathway. The good news is that you can be one with this Spirit—guided by this invisible force that positively shapes our thoughts words and deeds. Today a loving, omnipotent, omnipresent God of the universe can indwell and can make one's soul truly sing.

Your word is a lamp to my feet and a light for my path. Psalm 119:105

SOUL BE FREE

I'VE COME FOR A TIME
TO THIS PLACE
MY BODY A COVERING
TO RUN THIS RACE
KNOWING MY SOUL
MUST BE FREE
MOMENTS SPENT
LIGHT SHINES THROUGH ME
I'VE COME FOR A TIME
SOUL MUST BE FREE
THIS JOURNEY HOME
SEED DEEP IN ME
MY PATH, MY COURSE
NOT IN MY HAND
SOUL BE FREE GOD'S
MASTER PLAN
STEP FROM THIS WORLD
A WORD TO GIVE
MY LIGHT MY LOVE
MY
SPIRIT
LIVES.

There is a place deep down in our soul that longs for the eternal. It is this longing that beckons us closer to becoming an expression of God's love. Our sole purpose in the earth is to bring glory to the Creator. When we surrender our will to the will of God we release a light that shines in and beyond this earthly realm. Each life experience marks the path that leads to our ultimate journey home.

Now we know that if the tent we live in is destroyed, we have a building from God, an eternal house in heaven not built by hands.
2 Corinthians 5:1

THE BENEDICTION

As we continue on our life journey we beseech you Oh God to touch our mind, touch our relationships and bring understanding to the issues that mire us in spirit-consuming situations. God be with us through the dark days of anger, depression and frustration. We need your power to transform old thought patterns inconsistent with your will for our lives. Let us find a safe harbor in you where change is no longer scary or something to be avoided. Free us from the strongholds that once ruled over every aspect of our being. We ask that you be our daily bread and feed us until we want no more. Guide us on the inward journey in order to be authentic to ourselves, to others and to you. Give us power to think new and liberating thoughts through the process of spiritual revelation and uncompromising self-awareness. Lift us from the depths of ordinariness to the heights of extraordinary faith, extraordinary love and the extraordinary power to teach, reach and nurture others. Immanuel, as we move from this place we thank you because we can now hear over the empty noise of the world, your still small voice encouraging urgently and lovingly... Soul Be Free. Amen

SCRIPTURES
from the NIV Bible
unless otherwise indicated

THE MIND

1-PROVERBS 19:8
2-PSALM 139:7-10
3-JEREMIAH 29:11 (AMP)
4-2 TIMOTHY 1:7 (NKJV)
5-ROMANS 12:2 (NKJV)

THE ISSUES

6-2 CORINTHIANS 4:7 (KJV)
7-EPHESIANS 2:10
8-ISAIAH 40:31
9-PSALM 27:14 (NKJV)
10-JOHN 15:5

THE RELATIONSHIP

11-PSALM 19:1
12-1 CORINTHIANS
13-PROVERBS 17:17
14-PSALM 71:18
15-HABAKKUK 2:3
16-MATTHEW 6:11

THE SOUL

17-PROVERBS 3:5,6 (NKJV)
18-PSALM 121:1,2
19-1 JOHN 1:5b
20-PSALM 119:105
21-2 CORINTHIANS 5:1

ALFONSO WYATT is a renowned public theologian, role model, mentor and national speaker on issues that impact children, youth, families and community health. He is an advisor to government, universities, public schools, community-based organizations and civic groups. He is an Ordained Elder on the ministerial staff of The Greater Allen AME Cathedral of New York where he has designed innovative workshops and seminars for

Photo courtesy: Jorg Windau

church leaders, men, youth ministries and married couples. Alfonso Wyatt attended Howard University, Columbia Teachers College, The Ackerman Institute for Family Therapy, Columbia Institute for Nonprofit Management, and New York Theological Seminary, serving as an adjunct professor and program advisor. He is Chair of the Black Leadership Commission on AIDS New York City Affiliate and Chair of The 21st Century Foundation designed to increase philanthropy in the African-American community.

You shall receive power when the Holy Ghost comes upon you...

OUIDA WYATT is a Psalmist, artist and writer on the ministerial staff of The Greater Allen AME Cathedral of New York. She has served as an advisor, speaker and facilitator for Chosen Vessels Girl's Rite of Passage, The Cancer Support Ministry and Marriage Enrichment Ministry. Ouida Wyatt designed and taught a course titled *The Power of The Pen: Spiritual Growth Through Journaling.* She is a graduate of the College of New Rochelle, with a B.A. in Psychology. Ouida Wyatt states that her ministry is helping people discover inner peace, power and happiness through a deeper relationship with God and self. Alfonso and Ouida are partners in marriage and ministry for 35 years.

For we have this treasure in earthen vessels...

Notes

Notes

Notes